ENERGY
Now and in the Future

Geothermal Power

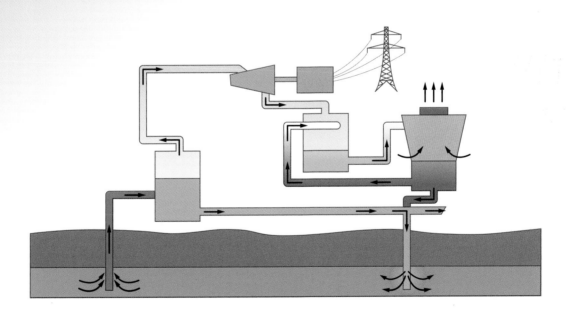

Neil Morris

Smart Apple Media

Smart Apple Media
P.O. Box 3263
Mankato, MN 56002

Printed in the United States of America

Library of Congress Cataloging-in-Publication Data

Morris, Neil, 1946-
  Geothermal power / by Neil Morris.
      p. cm. -- (Energy now and in the future)
  Includes index.
  ISBN 978-1-59920-340-9 (h)
  1. Geothermal resources--Juvenile literature. I. Title.
  GB1199.5.M67 2010
  333.8'8--dc22

                                                                2008050438

Designed by Helen James
Edited by Mary-Jane Wilkins
Artwork by Guy Callaby
Picture research by Su Alexander

Photograph acknowledgements
Page 8 Corbis; 11 Arctic- Images/Corbis; 12 Kennan Ward/Corbis; 13 Roger
Ressmeyer/Corbis; 15 Steven Vidler/Eurasia Press/Corbis; 17 Catherine Karnow/
Corbis; 18 Kevin R Morris/Corbis; 19 Atlantide Phototravel/Corbis; 21 Paul Souders/
Corbis; 22 Roger Ressmeyer/Corbis; 23 Arctic-Images/Corbis; 24 Annette
Soumillard/Hemis/Corbis; 30 Roger Ressmeyer/Corbis; 31 Bob Rowan; Progressive
Image/Corbis; 33 Geopower Basel AG;Fischer & Ryser; 35 Raymond Gehman/
Corbis; 37 Michael S Yamashita/Corbis; 38 Gary Braasch/Corbis; 39 Mark Newham;
Eye Ubiquitous/Corbis; 41 Barbara Walton/epa/Corbis; 42 Chenahotsprings.com
Front cover Annette Soumillard/Hemis/Corbis

9 8 7 6 5 4 3 2 1

Contents

Heat from Underground

The origins of geothermal energy are deep inside Earth. The word geothermal comes from the Greek words *ge* (meaning Earth) and *therme* (heat). The energy is produced by the planet's natural heat. Geothermal energy exists all over the world, and in many regions it can be used in large quantities. Experts believe it could be a very important energy source for the future.

Beneath the Crust

The inside of our planet is made up of four sections. If we could travel to Earth's center, we would notice the temperature increasing throughout our journey. We live on Earth's hard outer layer, called the crust, which acts as the planet's skin. The thickness of the crust varies from a depth of about 25 miles (40 km) under the continents to 5 miles (8 km) under the oceans.

The crust is made of different types of rocks. If we could bore our way down, we would find that the temperature increases by about 54°F per mile for the first 6 miles (30°C per km for the first 10 km). This shows how much heat is stored beneath the surface. Rock is a very poor conductor of heat, but the crust acts as a form of insulation, keeping much of the heat inside the planet.

From Mantle to Core

Beneath Earth's crust is a 1,800 mile (2,900 km) thick layer of mainly molten rock, called the mantle. This makes up more than three-fourths of the planet's volume. The temperature of the mantle increases to between 1290 and 1650°F (700 and 900°C) in the upper part. It increases to more than 7200°F (4000°C) at the bottom.

This cutaway illustration shows the four different sections that make up Earth's interior. The numbers give the diameter of the inner core and the width of the other three layers. The total distance from Earth's surface to its center is about 4,000 miles (6,500 km).

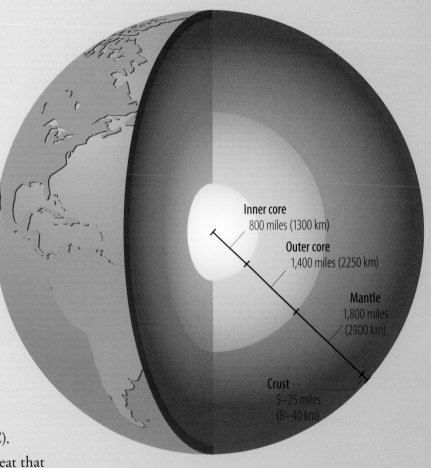

Inner core
800 miles (1300 km)

Outer core
1,400 miles (2250 km)

Mantle
1,800 miles
(2900 km)

Crust
5–25 miles
(8–40 km)

The molten rock moves very slowly, carrying heat toward Earth's surface, cooling and sinking to heat up again. The rock sinks toward Earth's outer core of two layers (molten iron and nickel). The outer core is about 1,400 miles (2,250 km) thick. Its temperature can be 11,000°F (6,000°C). Beneath this layer, the pressure is so great that the metal—which is mainly iron—is solid. This iron sphere is about 1,600 miles (2,600 km) across—just a little bigger than the moon. The temperature may be as high as 12,600 °F (7,000°C), which is hotter than the surface of the Sun.

Why Is Earth Hot Inside?

There are several reasons for this. Heat was left over when the planet was formed about 4.6 billion years ago. After the Sun formed, gas and dust spinning around it collided and stuck together, making planets, including Earth. The creation of Earth caused friction and this made it a hot molten ball that is still cooling. The denser, heavier parts sank toward the center of the planet, creating more friction and more heat. Since then, radioactive elements (such as uranium) in Earth's mantle and crust have been releasing energy particles in a process called radioactive decay. This process gives off huge amounts of energy in the form of heat, and this makes up most of today's geothermal energy.

A fountain of lava spurts out of Kilauea volcano, on the island of Hawaii. This huge volcano appears above a hot spot in Earth's crust (see page 11).

Letting out the Heat

Earth's solid, rocky crust keeps the planet's heat in. It is not completely sealed because the crust is not made of one continuous layer of rocks. It is cracked into huge pieces called tectonic plates (from the Greek word *tekton*, meaning builder). The plates fit together like a giant jigsaw puzzle. Heat rises into the crust through the upper part of the mantle, called the asthenosphere, on which the plates sit. The magma (or molten mantle rock) cools and slowly sinks again over millions of years. At the same time, the moving magma shifts the tectonic plates. Plates move very slowly—a few inches a year.

Piping Hot

An American geology professor has calculated that, on average, enough heat comes up through Earth's crust to make three cups of hot coffee every minute for the world's 6.7 billion inhabitants. That is 1.2 trillion cups of coffee every hour!

Volcanic World

As Earth's plates move, they rub against each other. This squeezing and buckling of plates can create volcanoes. These are openings in Earth's crust where magma forces its way through cracks to the surface. The streams of molten rock that reach the surface are called lava. Many volcanoes are caused when an oceanic plate is forced under a neighboring continental plate. This occurs in a convergent or destructive margin in a region known as a subduction zone. Forces cause cracks in the continental crust that become

Will Earth's Heat Ever Run Out?

Yes, it will, but not for a very long time. Earth, and especially the mantle, have been losing heat for some time, but in tiny amounts. At the same time, the planet's solid inner core expands very slowly (some scientists say by about 0.4 inches (1 cm) every thousand years). Geologists believe that the core's expansion is releasing more heat into the mantle.

Nevertheless, the overall cooling will continue by tiny amounts for billions of years. The cooling will harden the asthenosphere and tectonic plates may stop moving. But before it cools completely, in approximately another 5 billion years, Earth will have stopped receiving energy from the Sun, which will cool and swell up into a red giant star.

volcanoes. As the descending plate slips into the asthenosphere, its rocks melt back into the mantle and are recycled. The huge forces often produce massive earthquakes.

The Ultimate Energy Source

All our energy comes from the Sun, which makes it the ultimate energy source. This is also true for geothermal energy, because Earth would not have formed (and would not have been hot) if its original material had not been sent spinning around a new star— the Sun. Without the Sun, there would also be no weather on Earth and, therefore, no water cycle. Without water, we would not be able to use geothermal energy in the way we do—for heating or generating electricity.

A map of the world's major tectonic plates. The arrows show the direction in which the plates generally move. At a transform margin, the plates slide past one another.

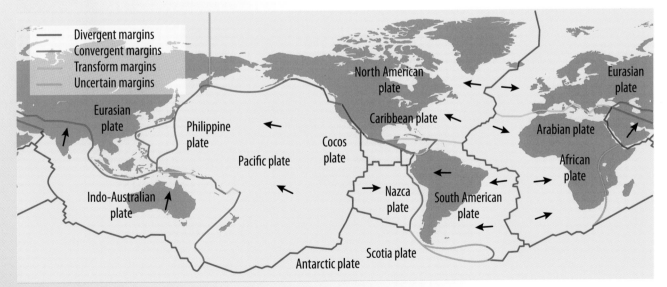

Divergent margins
Convergent margins
Transform margins
Uncertain margins

Eurasian plate
Philippine plate
Pacific plate
Cocos plate
Indo-Australian plate
Nazca plate
North American plate
Caribbean plate
South American plate
Arabian plate
African plate
Eurasian plate
Antarctic plate
Scotia plate

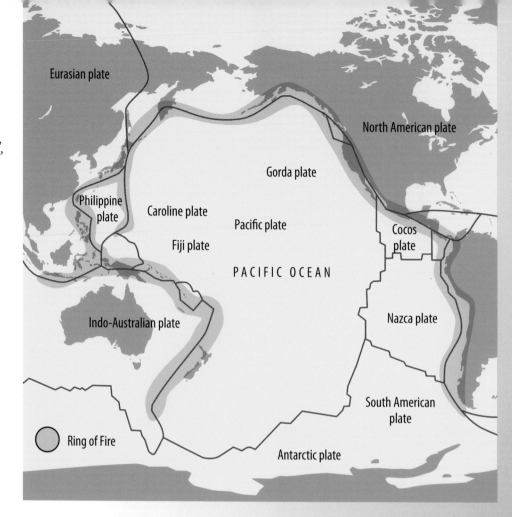

The Ring of Fire runs around the Pacific Ocean. Because of the enormous forces involved, the entire region experiences earthquakes as well as volcanoes.

Eurasian plate

North American plate

Gorda plate

Philippine plate

Caroline plate

Pacific plate

Cocos plate

Fiji plate

PACIFIC OCEAN

Indo-Australian plate

Nazca plate

South American plate

Ring of Fire

Antarctic plate

Ring of Fire

The main volcanic regions of the world are all near the edge of plates. These regions can produce the most geothermal power, as Earth's heat rises to the surface at these points. Many of them lie in a huge belt around the edges of the Pacific Ocean. This is known as the Ring of Fire and runs around the boundaries of the huge Pacific plate. To the west, the Ring of Fire runs from Japan down through the islands of southeast Asia to New Zealand. On the other side of the ocean, the Ring of Fire runs from Alaska down the length of the North American coast to the Andes mountains of South America. There are subduction zones on both sides of the ocean.

Making New Crust

As well as crashing together, plates can move apart. This occurs beneath the oceans and leaves a crack where magma comes to the surface, cools, hardens, and creates new crust. This process creates more than 0.77 square miles (2 sq km) of new ocean crust every year in regions called divergent or constructive margins. The areas of new hardened magma are known as spreading ridges.

Sometimes, the peaks of a ridge appear above the ocean surface and form islands. The best examples lie on the Mid-Atlantic Ridge, which stretches for about 10,000 miles (16,000 km) from northeast of Greenland to level with the southern tip of South America. Islands on the North Atlantic stretch of the ridge include Iceland and the Azores, both of which have large amounts of geothermal energy. In Iceland, the two plates move apart at about 0.8 inches (2 cm) per year.

Plumes and Hot Spots

Plates often move by about 4 inches (10 cm) every year. You can see this in parts of the world where hot, molten rocks come near to the surface and are called mantle plumes. They form areas called hot spots. As a plate moves over the spot (which is stationary) magma burns through the thin crust and creates a volcano. This movement causes a series of volcanoes. The Hawaiian islands were created in this way.

Drilling Through the Crust

Scientists have learned about geothermal heat from drilling projects. One day, it may be possible to drill to the mantle and tap into its intense heat. As of now, the deepest drilled hole is the Kola Superdeep Borehole in northwest Russia. Drilling began in 1970. By 1983, it had reached 39,000 feet (12,000 m). Six years later, the drill reached 40,230 feet (12,262 m)—the world's record. At that depth, the temperature was 356°F (180°C), which was higher than the expected 212°F (100°C). Drilling stopped in 1992. The hole went about one-third of the way into the continental crust, drilling into hot rocks that are about 2.7 billion years old. Future projects might concentrate on oceanic crust, which is generally much thinner.

This photograph of the Mid-Atlantic Ridge in Thingvellir National Park in Iceland clearly shows where two plates are slowly moving apart.

Old Faithful geyser, in Yellowstone National Park, Wyoming, erupts every 60–90 minutes. This region's geysers are popular with tourists, who have to keep a safe distance away from the hot water and steam.

Hot Springs and Geysers

The water in hot springs (also called thermal springs) is heated by hot molten rock that lies near the surface. Cold rainwater trickles down through cracks until it reaches rocks that have been heated up by magma. The hot, steaming water rises back up to the surface, where it may form a warm pool or stream. Some springs build up a great force in deep channels, where the hot water cannot easily boil and turn to steam because of the weight of cooler water above it (increased pressure raises the boiling point of a liquid). The channels are often 6,500 feet (2,000 m) deep.

When it eventually boils, the steam rises quickly and forces hot water, steam, and air ahead of it. Jets of steam and boiling water explode out of a crack or hole. The most explosive ones shoot water more than 330 feet (100 m) into the air. The jet of water lasts for a few seconds before the crack fills up and the process begins again.

Icelandic Gusher

Geysers are named after the Great Geysir in Iceland, which was probably first reported in the fourteenth century. In Icelandic, *geysir* means "gusher." The original geyser erupted every hour until the early twentieth century when it stopped. Earthquakes in 2000 reactivated the geyser and it now gushes every 8–10 hours, reaching a height of 200 feet (61 m).

Power versus Beauty

Many of the volcanic regions of the world with hot springs and geysers form beautiful landscapes. Some are national parks and have become important tourist attractions. The most famous is Yellowstone National Park, in northwest Wyoming. The U.S. National Park Service says that the 3,475 square mile (9,000 sq km) park has more geothermal features than any other place on Earth: "With half of the Earth's geothermal features, Yellowstone holds the planet's most diverse and intact collection of geysers, hot springs, mud pots, and fumaroles. Its more than 300 geysers make up two-thirds of all those found on Earth. Combine this with more than 10,000 thermal features, comprised of brilliantly colored hot springs, bubbling mud pots, and steaming fumaroles, and you have a place like no other."

Yellowstone became the first U.S. national park in 1872 when 300 people visited. Just over a hundred years later, it was made a World Heritage Site by the United Nations. Since 1990, almost 3 million tourists have visited the park every year. It would be difficult to use the geothermal energy of the region without spoiling the landscape and the pleasure of millions of people.

Fumaroles and Mud Pots

Fumaroles are holes in the ground that give off steam and gases such as carbon dioxide and hydrogen sulfide. When steam forces its way to the surface through layers of volcanic ash and clay, it may bubble and drop in a mud pot. Large areas of fumaroles and mud pots are in volcanic regions of Iceland, New Zealand, and the United States—including Yellowstone National Park.

Fumaroles spout gases on the Italian island of Vulcano, near Sicily. The name originated from the Roman god of fire, Vulcan, who also gave his name to volcanoes.

From Ancient Baths to Modern Spas

Scientists did not truly understand plate tectonics and how Earth's interior worked until the early twentieth century. Yet long before then, people were taking advantage of Earth's heat by using geothermal steam and hot springs for bathing and heating.

Ancient Greek Ideas

The Greek philosopher Empedocles (495–435 B.C.) believed that the world was made up of four elements—air, earth, fire, and water. The element of fire brought about volcanoes. Plato (427–347 B.C.) had slightly different ideas. He said that rivers of hot and cold water flowed through subterranean channels where there was also fire, mud, and lava. Aristotle (384–322 B.C.) thought that air was sucked into caves and was heated by underground fires. Eventually, the hot air was forced to the surface, causing volcanoes and earthquakes. The ancient Greek philosophers were on the right track, but they knew nothing of tectonic activity.

Earth Gods and Goddesses

People of many different cultures worshipped Earth and its life-giving forces. The ancient Egyptians honored Geb as an Earth deity and father of the gods. In ancient Greece and Rome, the Earth deity was female. The Greek Gaia was the daughter of Chaos, and Roman Tellus was also known as Terra Mater, or Mother Earth.

Roman Baths

The ancient Romans were the first to use hot springs to supply bathing houses. One of their famous baths was built in England. Historians believe that the Romans may have come across a warm spring that had earlier been a sacred place to Celtic Britons, who worshipped Sulis, the Celtic goddess of healing. The Romans called their settlement Aquae Sulis (waters of Sulis).

The Roman thermal bath house at Bath, in western England, is overlooked by a later Christian abbey.

Around A.D. 65 they built a temple dedicated to their goddess of medicine and wisdom, Minerva. They also constructed a lead-lined stone chamber around the sacred spring and a large rectangular bath, which was fed by the spring's warm waters. The Romans later included a caldarium (hot bath), tepidarium (warm bath), and frigidarium (cold bath). These are now part of the city of Bath, England.

Thermal Bathing Today

People still believe that thermal bathing is good for them. Some doctors think that the warmth and mineral properties of thermal water can help treat rheumatic disorders, skin ailments, and respiratory problems. In Bath, you can visit the Roman baths, although you can no longer bathe in them. In 2006, a complex of thermal baths opened in a new building. The operators say: "Thermae Bath Spa is a day spa where you can bathe in the warm, natural, mineral-rich waters and choose from a range of spa treatments designed to ease the body and soothe the mind. The water from these springs is believed to have fallen as rain around 10,000 years ago and then sank to a depth of about two kilometers [1 mile] below the Earth's surface. It was heated by high-temperature rocks before rising back up through a break in the limestone that lies beneath the city of Bath. More than one million liters of mineral-rich water flow from the thermal springs each day, at an average temperature of 45°C [113°F]."

Taking the Cure

People who believed that thermal waters could help with medical problems began "taking the cure" by visiting hot springs. The small village of Barèges, 4,000 feet (1,250 m) up in the Pyrenees Mountains of southwestern France, became a cure resort during the seventeenth century. This was two centuries after a farmer found an injured sheep bathing in a warm pool and noticed that the animal recovered well from its injuries. We now know that hot thermal waters rise to the surface at Barèges along a fault line between two different kinds of rock—granite and schist. The waters became more widely known in 1675 when members of the French royal family went to the village to bathe in hot baths and mud that was rich in sulfur and other minerals. During the nineteenth century, the thermal baths became part of a hospital that treated war wounds, rheumatism, and skin problems.

Bathing for Health

Medical treatment in thermal springs came to be known as balneotherapy (from the Latin *balnium*, meaning bath), or medicinal bathing. Although many people have reported pain relief from balneotherapy, scientific studies have not been able to prove that the therapy is as effective as some claim.

Spa Resorts

Many European towns began to specialize in offering cures at their baths. Some, such as Aachen and Baden-Baden in Germany, became more famous than Barèges. Another was the small Belgian town of Spa, in the Ardennes hills near Liège. The town had been known for its hot springs since the fourteenth century. It became so famous that by 1600 the word spa was used to describe any resort with mineral springs. Bath, for example, became known as a spa, and the term is now in general use.

Native American Springs

There are many hot springs in North and South America. Archaeologists have found evidence that Native Americans used the hot springs thousands of years ago for warm bathing and perhaps as a

Swimmers enjoy the thermal pool of the Gellert bath in Budapest, the capital of Hungary. The city has 188 thermal springs. This bath opened in 1918.

source of healing. The different tribes probably saw springs as neutral regions where they could live and bathe together in peace. One such place was Tonopah in Arizona, which was named by the early Hohokam people and means "hot water under the bush." The springs came from a large underground source.

Have Hot Springs Always Had a Positive Image?

Not really, because some people have associated them with natural disasters, such as volcanic eruptions and earthquakes. Historians believe that the Native Americans of the California region bathed in the local hot springs for their health and possibly as part of a ritual ceremony. But when the explorer William Bell Elliot came upon a steaming valley of Californian fumaroles in 1847, he reported that he had discovered the "gates of hell." He called the region the Geysers (though what he had found were fumaroles). This eventually became the largest complex of geothermal power plants in the world (see page 30).

American Resorts

During the 1850s, the Geysers was developed into a spa with a resort hotel. In 1862, a rich businessman named Samuel Brannan (1819–89) opened another resort nearby, which he called Calistoga. There was a luxury hotel, with bathhouses for rich guests, and soon there was railroad service from San Francisco. One of the most famous spa visitors was writer Robert Louis Stevenson. In 1881, Calistoga made headlines in national newspapers when Anson Tichenor claimed he had invented a way to extract gold from its hot springs. Unfortunately for Tichenor and Brannan, the invention was a fraud.

The Idaho State Capitol building in the city of Boise is heated by a geothermal well. The building was completed in 1920.

Do Springs Ever Dry Up?

If there is a good source of rainwater seeping into the natural reservoir, this is unlikely. However, geological changes and rock movements can change underground formations. If too much hot water and steam are taken out through man-made boreholes, underground reserves can fall. Around Larderello, Italy, experts found that steam pressure had fallen. Underground reserves of thermal water have dropped by nearly one-third since the 1950s. This has led the energy company responsible for the area to drill twice as deep, 69–13,000 feet (21–4,000 m) below ground, to find hotter sources.

Heating for Homes

During the nineteenth century, American engineers worked on ways of using geothermal water and steam. In 1892, a water company in Boise, Idaho, offered to supply houses with hot water from two geothermal wells just outside the city. The company also built a geothermally heated indoor swimming pool. Within a few years, the system was supplying

Francesco Larderel

French-born entrepreneur Francesco Larderel (1789–1858) set up a plant to extract a chemical called boric acid in a region of hot springs near the Tuscan city of Siena, in northern Italy. At first, Larderel burned wood as fuel to boil water and volcanic mud from the springs, which contained a form of the mineral boron. Then, in 1827, he developed a way of using geothermal steam instead of burning wood. Before long, he was able to use the steam to drive well drills and pumps. This was the first time geothermal power was used for industrial purposes. Today, there is a Geothermal Museum in Larderello, the town named after the entrepreneur, which commemorates his pioneering work.

There is still a geothermal plant at Larderello, Italy.

200 homes and many businesses. A similar system still operates in Boise and extracts nearly 607.6 thousand gallons (2.3 billion L) of geothermal water at a temperature of about 154°F (68°C).

First Geothermal Electricity

The chemical works at Larderello continued after the founder's death. In 1904, there was a fundamental change in the way the region used geothermal energy. The head of the company, Prince Piero Ginori Conti, used steam from the fumaroles to drive a dynamo (or simple generator) that produced enough electricity to illuminate five light bulbs. This may not seem to be very much, but it demonstrated that geothermal electricity was a possibility. It led to the development of a larger electrical plant a few years later at a nearby site known as Devil's Valley.

Geothermal Heating

We can use hot water from geothermal springs in heating systems. This is a direct use of geothermal power. The thermal water circulates through pipes, just as heated water does in a heating system fired by oil or gas. The thermal water also can be used to heat cold water for the same purpose. This system is used when the thermal water contains such a high level of minerals that it would clog up water pipes.

Who Uses Geothermal Power?

Geothermal heating systems can be used in homes and for many industrial purposes. Many countries use geothermal energy directly. The chart shows the biggest users and includes their percentage of world use. These figures are slightly misleading. The United States and China are huge countries with large populations (China has more than 1.3 billion people). At the other end of the scale, Iceland has 0.3 million people and Switzerland has 7.6 million. This means that Iceland produces the most geothermal energy per person —68 times more than Switzerland, which is second in the per person list. Hungary is third, Sweden fourth, and the United States fifth.

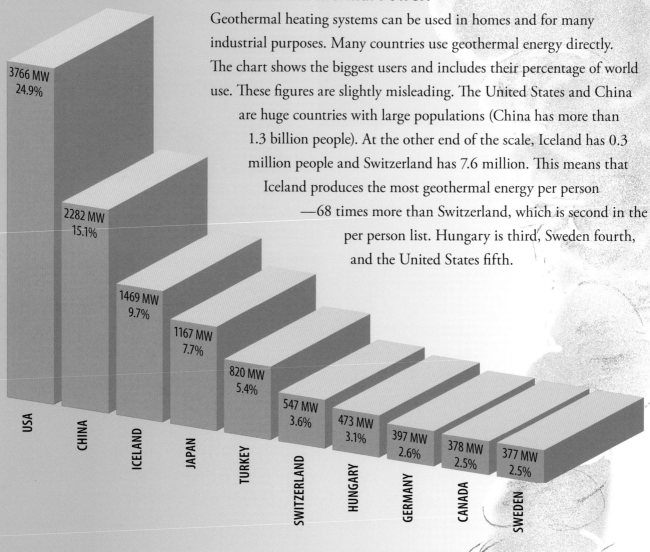

USA — 3766 MW / 24.9%
CHINA — 2282 MW / 15.1%
ICELAND — 1469 MW / 9.7%
JAPAN — 1167 MW / 7.7%
TURKEY — 820 MW / 5.4%
SWITZERLAND — 547 MW / 3.6%
HUNGARY — 473 MW / 3.1%
GERMANY — 397 MW / 2.6%
CANADA — 378 MW / 2.5%
SWEDEN — 377 MW / 2.5%

Land of Fire and Ice

The people who first settled on the island of Iceland, around 870, called their main settlement Reykjavik, which means "smoky bay." They saw what they thought was smoke coming out of the ground, but this was steam from hot springs and fumaroles. Today, tourist operators call Iceland the "land of fire and ice." The island lies just below the Arctic Circle and has many icy glaciers, but it is also an active volcanic region. According to ancient records, people used hot springs for washing and bathing. The first man-made wells for collecting hot water were sunk in 1756. By 1930, a school, a hospital, and 60 homes were heated in Reykjavik with thermal water.

Why Does Iceland Have so Much Geothermal Power?

Iceland is special in terms of geothermal activity. It is a volcanic island with more than 200 active volcanoes and 600 hot springs. As the Icelandic Tourist Board states: "Situated on the Mid-Atlantic Ridge, Iceland is a hot spot of volcanic and geothermal activity: 30 post-glacial volcanoes have erupted in the past two centuries, and natural hot water supplies much of the population with cheap, pollution-free heating." There is plenty of thermal water that flows at a fast rate. The Icelandic hot spring Deildartunguhver has Europe's highest flow rate of 47.5 gallons (180 L) per second and provides water at 207°F (97°C), which is piped up to 40 miles (64 km) to heat towns and villages.

Large pipes lead from a geothermal plant in New Zealand, which uses almost as much direct thermal heating as Sweden (see the chart opposite).

21

Hotter and Cooler Areas

Geothermal areas in Iceland are divided into high- and low-temperature fields. The dividing point is 302°F (150°C). High-temperature fields measure at least 302°F (150°C) at a depth of 3,280 feet (1,000 m) and are in the active volcanic zone. This runs along the tectonic plate boundaries of the Mid-Atlantic Ridge (see page 11). Hot magma chambers supply the fumaroles, mud pots, and hot springs. The water temperature rises to 662°F (350°C) at about 6,560 feet (2,000 m) below ground. The Nesjavellir high-temperature field produces water at 482–572°F (250–300°C). Experts have identified 28 high-temperature fields in Iceland, as well as 250 low-temperature fields.

Building up a System

During the 1930s, engineers drilled 32 boreholes in a geothermal area about 10.5 miles (17 km) east of Reykjavik. By 1940, engineers were laying a pipeline from the boreholes to the capital and building a large storage tank for the thermal water, which had a temperature of 187°F (86°C). By the 1950s, half of

Steam rises from a pipeline near the Nesjavellir geothermal plant in Iceland.

What Is it Used For?

People in Iceland use geothermal energy for:

Space heating (homes)	57.4%
Electricity generation	15.9%
Fish farming	10.4%
Snow melting	5.4%
Industry	4.7%
Swimming pools	3.7%
Greenhouses	2.5%

Reykjavik's citizens had access to hot geothermal water. More boreholes were sunk in other areas. By 1972, nearly everyone had geothermal heating.

How the Reykjavik System Works

Hot water is pumped out of boreholes from about 656 feet (200 m) underground by electric motors. The water is pumped through 35-inch (90-cm) wide pipes and flows downhill to the city's six storage tanks. Then it is pumped through narrower pipes to districts, streets, and individual homes. Customers' hot water use is measured by their water meters. The water passes through radiators and into hot-water tanks and taps for washing and bathing. Most of the used water flows into rainwater drains. Some heating water is returned to a pumping station and is mixed with very hot water to bring it to a working temperature of 176°F (80°C).

Cutting Pollution

Using geothermal power can help to reduce air pollution. Before the mid-twentieth century, the main source of heat and power in Reykjavik was coal. Burning coal gave off so much waste gas that a cloud of black smoke often hung over the city. This air pollution added to the greenhouse effect that is causing global warming (see page 35). In 1960, about 275,575 tons (250,000 t) of CO_2 were sent into the atmosphere just by heating Reykjavik. By 1975, this amount was reduced to about 22,000 tons (20,000 t) a year. Today, it is virtually nil.

Melting Snow and Ice

Once the hot water has traveled through a heating system, it is 77–104°F (25–40°C). In winter, some of it is pumped into tanks and pipes to clear roads and sidewalks of snow and ice. In Reykjavik, the average temperature is 30°F (-1°C) in January and 52°F (11°C) in July. Heating is needed all year round.

The city of Reykjavik, on the southwest coast of Iceland, lies next to snow-covered mountains.

The Blue Lagoon

One of the world's most popular geothermal spots is a lake of waste water from an Icelandic power plant. The plant in southwest Iceland lies above a large geothermal reservoir. Salt water seeps into the reservoir from the nearby sea. The plant has wells up to 6,500 feet (2,000 m) deep that produce steam and 125 gallons (475 L) per second of 194°F (90°C) hot water. This drives turbines and produces electricity, before passing through an exchanger to heat water to heat nearby communities. Finally, the water passes into a large pool known as the Blue Lagoon. It looks blue because of microscopic algae in the water. By then the water is about 104°F (40°C), a pleasant temperature for bathing. The warm water is rich in silica, sulfur, and other minerals. The lagoon has become a health resort as well as a bathing pool. People claim that the water is especially soothing for skin problems.

Good for You?

The Blue Lagoon operators claim that their mineral-rich waters are very healthy. They encourage visitors to apply the volcanic mud at the bottom of the pool to their bodies. Their web site states: "Guests enjoy bathing and relaxing in Blue Lagoon geothermal seawater, known for its positive effects on the skin. A visit to the spa promotes harmony between body, mind, and spirit, and enables one to soak away the stresses of modern life. The spa's guests rekindle their relationship with nature, soak up the scenic beauty, and enjoy breathing the clean, fresh air."

Bathers enjoy the warm geothermal waters of the Blue Lagoon in Iceland.

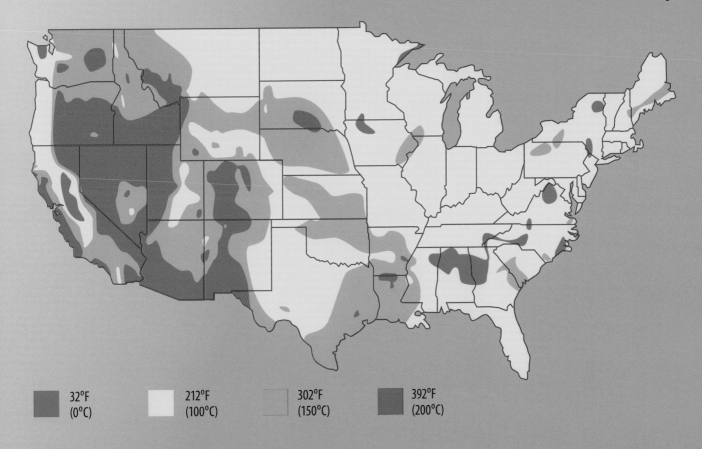

■ 32°F (0°C)	■ 212°F (100°C)	■ 302°F (150°C)	■ 392°F (200°C)

World's Largest Producer

The United States produces nearly one-quarter of the world's geothermal power for direct use. As the map shows, most geothermal areas are in the west. According to the U.S. Department of Energy, a recent survey of western states found more than 9,000 thermal wells and springs, more than 900 low- to moderate-temperature geothermal areas, and hundreds of direct-use sites. The survey identified 271 western towns and communities with a total population of 7.4 million within 5 miles (8 km) of a usable geothermal site. Experts calculate that if geothermal resources were used to heat buildings in the 271 communities, 18 million barrels of oil would be saved each year.

A map produced by the U.S. Department of Energy shows estimated underground temperatures in the United States at a depth of 3.7 miles (6 km).

Farmers and Gardeners

Geothermal energy is particularly useful for farmers and gardeners. Hot-water pipes provide heat for greenhouses and can heat the soil in the fields. This allows growers to cultivate vegetables, flowers, and tree seedlings out of season or in a cold climate. Fish farms use the warm water to breed tropical fish in cooler waters. In Idaho, one geothermal fish farm has some warm outdoor ponds for breeding alligators. The farm has no pumps, pipes, or heat exchangers, so the operating cost of the geothermal system is zero.

Pumping Heat

The top few feet of Earth's surface stay at a relatively constant temperature all year round. The ground is generally warmer than the air during winter, remaining at about 50–61°F (10–16°C). A geothermal heat pump takes advantage of this source of warmth by transferring it into a building. During the warm summer months, the system can work the other way by taking heat from the building and transferring it to the ground, which acts as a heat sink. The pump heats a building in winter and cools it in summer. It can also run a hot-water system.

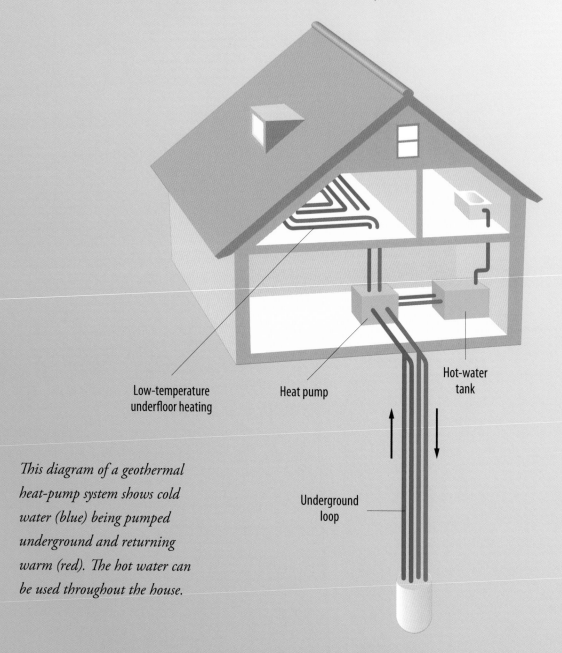

Low-temperature underfloor heating

Heat pump

Hot-water tank

Underground loop

This diagram of a geothermal heat-pump system shows cold water (blue) being pumped underground and returning warm (red). The hot water can be used throughout the house.

What's in a Name?

Geothermal heat pump (GHP) systems are also known as ground-source or ground-coupled heat pumps, water-source heat pumps (as opposed to air-source), or geothermal exchange systems. Many different companies sell and install the technology for homeowners, and some have their own trade names.

Looping Down

To pick up geothermal heat, a length of plastic pipe —called a loop—is buried in the ground near the building. The loop can be placed either vertically or horizontally. An antifreeze solution is pumped through the pipe by an electric pump. The antifreeze is heated by the ground as it passes through it on its way to the heat pump inside the building. This pump, which also runs on electricity, has a heat exchanger that takes heat from the solution to warm air that it pumps throughout the building. Alternatively, it can be used to pump warm water around a series of radiators. The cool antifreeze solution then flows back through the underground loop to pick up more heat.

Environmental Benefits

According to the Geothermal Heat Pump Consortium, GHPs have a huge effect on the environment. In the United States, there are more than 1 million GHP installations. This saves 21.5 million barrels of crude oil and cuts carbon dioxide emissions by 6.4 million tons (5.8 million t). In terms of reducing greenhouse gases, this is equivalent to taking nearly 1.3 million cars off the road or planting more than 385 million trees.

Are Heat Pumps Expensive?

The initial cost of installing a geothermal heat pump system can be two or three times more than a gas heating system. But the geothermal system cuts heating (and cooling) costs by 35–70 percent. This means that the system usually pays for itself in three to five years. The average lifespan of a pump is about 22 years, and loops should last at least 50 years.

As well as saving money, geothermal pumps have other advantages. The U.S. Environmental Protection Agency calls them "the most energy-efficient, environmentally clean, cost-effective space conditioning systems available." Geothermal pumps became popular in the 1980s and have become more appealing in the twenty-first century as the price of oil and gas continues to rise. Apart from a small amount of electricity, the heat pump uses geothermal energy.

Generating Electricity

Geothermal steam and hot water can drive generators and produce electricity as well as being used for heating systems. This technology was first introduced in Italy in 1904 (see page 19) and was developed around the world during the twentieth century. Today, geothermal electricity makes up less than 1 percent of total global production, but that still means that it supplies electricity to about 60 million people.

Turbines and Generators

Electricity generation began in the nineteenth century. In 1831, British scientist Michael Faraday (1791–1867) discovered that he could create electricity by moving a magnet through a coil of copper wire. This process is called electromagnetic induction. It led to the invention of the electric generator, which works by changing mechanical energy into electrical energy. In geothermal power plants, steam provides the mechanical energy by turning the rotor blades of a turbine. The blades are connected to a shaft, which is also attached to a generator. Inside the generator, the shaft makes magnets spin inside wire coils to produce electricity.

Top Ten

Compare this chart of the world's top geothermal electricity producers with the chart on page 20. Only three countries appear in both charts: the United States, Japan, and Iceland.

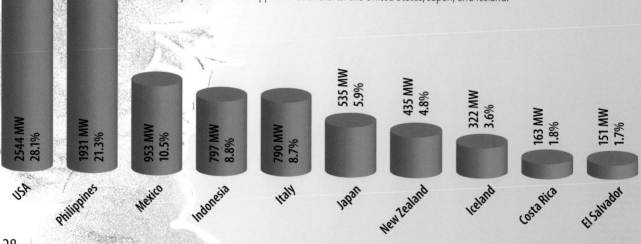

USA	2544 MW	28.1%
Philippines	1931 MW	21.3%
Mexico	953 MW	10.5%
Indonesia	797 MW	8.8%
Italy	790 MW	8.7%
Japan	535 MW	5.9%
New Zealand	435 MW	4.8%
Iceland	322 MW	3.6%
Costa Rica	163 MW	1.8%
El Salvador	151 MW	1.7%

FLASH-STEAM POWER PLANT

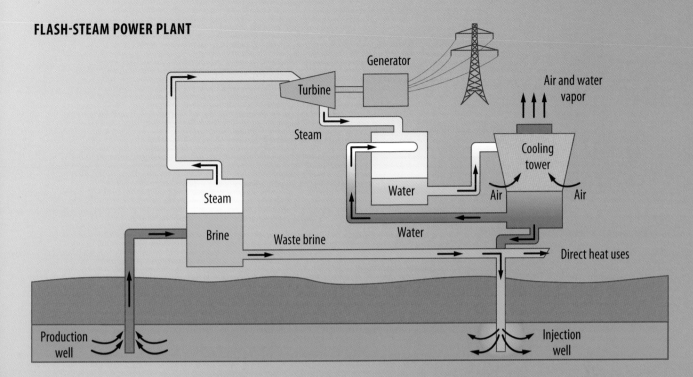

How the Power Plant Works

Steam power plants use geothermal steam and hot water. In dry steam plants, the steam comes directly from the geothermal source and is used to turn the turbine. Increased pressure raises a liquid's boiling point. This means water can be much hotter than 212°F (100°C) underground and still be a liquid. In a flash-steam power plant, very hot, high-pressure water is flashed (or depressurized) to produce steam. The steam then turns a turbine, which drives a generator to produce electricity.

In a flash-steam plant, as in other geothermal plants, heat is used both to produce electricity and for direct heating. Used water is returned underground so the well does not dry up.

Does Geothermal Power Pollute the Air?

Geothermal power plants emit mainly water vapor (as steam). This is a greenhouse gas but is not believed very damaging to the atmosphere. Some people worry about hydrogen sulfide (which smells like rotten eggs) found in all geothermal areas. Minute amounts of carbon dioxide, nitric oxide, and sulfur are emitted. There also may be other minerals released along with steam. The magazine *Renewable Energy World* says: "When it comes to the environmental benefits of using geothermal for power production, the majority of emissions from a geothermal source are water vapor. A coal plant with scrubbers and other emissions control technologies can emit 24 times more carbon dioxide, 10,837 times more sulfur dioxide, and 3,865 times more nitrous oxides per megawatt hour than a geothermal steam plant, according to the GEA [Geothermal Energy Association]."

29

A Two-Part System

Binary plants use a different system and are useful where there is a supply of hot geothermal water rather than steam. The hot water passes through a heat exchanger containing a fluid with a lower boiling point, such as isobutane. The fluid vaporizes, and the vapor turns the turbine, which drives the generator. The remaining secondary fluid is recycled through the heat exchanger. The geothermal water is returned to the reservoir. Binary plants are closed (or self-contained), so they do not emit gases.

World's Largest Power Plants

The biggest series of geothermal power plants in the world is in the Mayacamas Mountains, a 30 square mile (78 sq km) region of California, about 70 miles (115 km) north of San Francisco. The area is called the Geysers, and fumaroles were found there in the nineteenth century (see page 17). In 1921, America's first geothermal plant produced electricity to light the spa resort. In 1960, a large commercial plant opened at the Geysers, producing 11 MW of power. Today, 21 separate power plants use steam from more than 350 geothermal wells. They generate more than 725 MW of electricity—enough to power 725,000 homes across five California counties.

What Is a Watt?

A watt (W) is a unit of power that measures the rate of producing or using energy. The term was named after Scottish engineer James Watt (1736–1819), who developed an improved steam engine. Watt measured his engine's performance in horsepower (hp). One horsepower equals 746 watts. Today, watts are generally used to measure electric power.

1 kilowatt (kW) = 1 thousand watts
1 megawatt (MW) = 1 million watts
1 gigawatt (GW) = 1 billion watts

*One of the electric power plants
at the Geysers, California.*

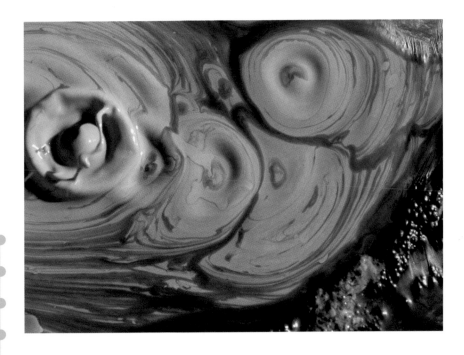

Mud pots bubble near one of the Geysers power plants.

From the Depths

Geological studies suggest that the heat source for the Geysers is an 8.6 foot (14 km) wide magma chamber that lies about 4.3 miles (7 km) beneath the surface. This volcanic region is connected to the famous San Andreas Fault, which is responsible for many earthquakes in California.

Recycling Power

The Geysers area was developed very rapidly in the 1980s. By 1990, the total capacity had increased to 2000 MW. As in other dry steam plants, some of the steam condenses to water after passing through the turbine and is returned below ground through a separate injection well. Nevertheless, around two-thirds of the steam goes up into the atmosphere, and the underground steam pressure has been steadily decreasing. Projects are under way to introduce more water to the underground reservoir.

Do Geothermal Plants Produce Electricity All the Time?

Hot springs and thermal wells produce heat continuously. In theory, geothermal power plants can generate electricity all the time. In practice, there is a small amount of downtime for servicing. As the environmental group Greenpeace states: "Geothermal power generation causes virtually no pollution or greenhouse gas emissions. It's also quiet, and extremely reliable. Geothermal power plants produce electricity about 90 percent of the time, compared to 65–75 percent for fossil fuel power plants. Unfortunately, even in many countries with abundant geothermal reserves, this proven renewable energy source is being massively underutilized."

GEOTHERMAL POWER

Hot Rocks

Scientists have been working for many years on technology known as hot dry rock (HDR). When geologists find a suitable area, engineers drill down to where the underground rocks are hot, but there is little or no water. Water is pumped down into this borehole (called an injection well), and this opens small cracks in the bed of hot rocks, making a thermal reservoir. Then engineers drill a second borehole, called a production well, so that the heated water returns to the surface, as it does in a natural geyser. The HDR pressurized hot water can be used to heat another liquid in a heat exchanger before it is returned underground through the injection well to regain its geothermal heat. Steam from the heat exchanger can drive a turbine and generate electricity in the same way as in other power plants.

American Research

American scientists began a research program in 1971 at Fenton Hill in the Jemez Mountains of New Mexico. Fenton Hill is the site of a dormant volcano that probably last erupted 60,000 years ago. Engineers drilled a borehole nearly 9,900 feet (3,000 m) deep into a bedrock of granite where the temperature was 387°F (197°C). In 1980, German and Japanese scientists joined the project and drilled a deeper borehole down to 14,403 feet (4,390 m) where the temperature was 621°F (327°C). They pumped water into the reservoir over several days and drilled a production well that proved that the technology worked. However, the project had finished by 1996, when the Fenton Hill site was closed. Nevertheless, the scientists learned a great deal about HDR.

This illustration shows how an HDR system works. Could this be the future for geothermal power?

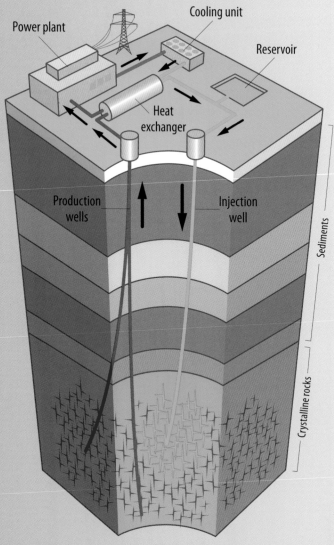

Power plant

Cooling unit

Reservoir

Heat exchanger

Production wells

Injection well

Sediments

Crystalline rocks

This is the drill derrick for the Swiss Deep Heat Mining project in Basel. Work was stopped after earth tremors were felt in Basel. A decision on further work depends on the outcome of investigations.

Swiss Tremors

The Deep Heat Mining project aims to set up a geothermal power plant in Basel, Switzerland, in the near future. The plant should be able to generate 20,000 megawatt-hours of electricity per year and 80,000 megawatt-hours of heating. In December 2006, engineers started pumping water into a 3.1 mile (5 km) deep borehole. Within days, a small earthquake was reported in the nearby city of Basel. The quake measured 3.4 on the Richter scale and caused minor damage to some buildings. Water pumping was stopped at once, but more tremors were felt later. People were particularly worried because Basel was flattened by a huge earthquake in 1356.

Is Geothermal Technology Dangerous?

It is not yet far enough advanced to answer this question. There is always an element of danger when engineers drill or mine underground because rocks move and fractures can cause tremors. Minor earthquakes have been caused by filling reservoirs with water, so it is possible that pumping water deep underground could also have this effect. The Basel incident confirmed this, and small tremors have been noted during other HDR programs, including the U.S. Fenton Hill project. Scientists have learned a great deal from these incidents, which should help to make the technology safer in the future.

Australian Granite

Scientists at the University of New South Wales began working on HDR in 1993. Since then, interest has grown throughout Australia, and 32 companies had applied for licenses to drill in geothermal areas by 2008. In the state of South Australia, 22 companies have applied for more than 200 licenses covering a geothermal area of more than 30,000 square miles (80,000 sq km). Two of the best areas are thought to be the Cooper Basin area of South Australia and the Hunter Valley of New South Wales. In 2008, one company reached a borehole depth of 13,852 feet (4,222 m) and hopes to produce HDR geothermal electricity in the near future.

Huge Research Costs

One of the problems with geothermal electricity is that HDR and similar technologies cost a great deal to research. Ideally, governments and international agencies would undertake research and development because individual companies do not want to spend the money without guaranteed rewards. The environmental group Envocare is convinced that more money needs to be spent: "Internationally the quantity of geothermal energy is virtually infinite and the environmental benefits are beyond reproach. Set against this are the disadvantages that considerably more research and development are needed to take advantage of the buried wealth, and even when a commercially viable site is identified,

Unlimited Heat Resource

The Australian energy company Geodynamics believes that Australia has large volumes of hot granite rocks between 1.9–3.1 miles (3–5 km) beneath the surface. The company believes that 0.24 cubic mile (1 cu km) of hot granite at 482°F (250°C) has the same amount of stored energy as 40 million barrels of oil. It states: "This represents a vast resource of clean energy that can potentially be tapped by hot fractured rock geothermal technology." Hot fractured rock (HFR) is another term for HDR and is called that because the injected water fractures, or further splits, tiny cracks in underground rocks.

Renewable Resource

Geothermal energy is called a renewable resource because we do not reduce stocks of it by using it. This means there is never any danger of the resource running out.

the initial investment cost can be a serious deterrent. Maybe if some of the multinationals that have the resources to invest in oil exploration could channel them into geothermal exploration, research, and development, we might see geothermal energy being tapped on a significant scale. But then we're prejudiced, aren't we?"

A geothermal expert takes a close look at a hot spring in Yellowstone National Park, Wyoming.

Geothermal Power and Global Warming

Earth's atmosphere prevents some of the Sun's rays from reaching Earth. Its gases also stop some heat escaping from Earth, just as glass traps warmth inside a greenhouse. We add to this natural greenhouse effect by emitting waste gases from power plants, factories, and cars. Many of these greenhouse gases —especially carbon dioxide—are produced when we burn coal, oil, or gas to release energy. Experts have discovered that in this way humans are making natural climate change more extreme. Much of our energy use adds to global warming, so land, sea, and air temperatures are gradually increasing. Using energy from renewable sources—such as geothermal energy—can help to reduce the increase in global warming.

Geothermal Energy Around the World

Geothermal energy—Earth's heat—comes through the planet's crust to its surface all over the world. This means that geothermal power can be tapped into from all the world's continents. However, there is much more accessible power in volcanic regions with a lot of tectonic activity, such as the Pacific rim known as the Ring of Fire (see page 10).

In the early twenty-first century, North America produces more electricity from geothermal sources than any other continent. Next is Asia, where the largest electricity producer is the Philippines, and the biggest direct user is China.

Island Countries

Geothermal power is growing fast in the island countries of southeast Asia. Research began in the Philippines in the 1970s, and the first commercial power plant began operating in 1977. Today, geothermal power generates one-fourth of the country's electricity, and there are plants on Luzon, Leyte, and other main islands with cables on the Pacific seabed to connect them. Geothermal heat is also used directly in the Philippines to process fish, dry fruit, and desalinate water (remove salt from seawater).

Farther south, Indonesia is also using more geothermal energy. In 2004, a total of 18 power plants produced 807 MW of geothermal power. This made up 60 percent of its power from renewable sources and 2 percent of its total power production. By 2025, Indonesia is aiming to have at least 13 more plants and to increase the geothermal total to 9,500 MW (44 percent of its renewable energy and 4 percent of the total).

Geothermal Power in Japan

The islands of Japan lie where four of the planet's tectonic plates meet—the Eurasian and North American plates to the north and the Philippine and Pacific plates to the south. So it is not surprising that Japan has many volcanoes and experiences about 1,000 earthquakes every year. Japan also has a long tradition of using its thermal resources. One city famous for its spas and bathhouses is Beppu, which has eight major hot springs. It has become a tourist attraction for Japanese and international visitors.

Japan began using geothermal electricity in 1966. By 1982, it had seven geothermal power plants. One of the problems in Japan is that the hot springs are in areas that have become national parks. This makes it difficult for industry to develop further. Environmentalists understandably oppose development in these areas, but this means that renewable resources cannot be fully exploited.

Bathing at a thermal pool in Beppu, Japan.

Tapping Potential Energy

Geological researchers in southeast Asia are certain there is much more geothermal energy to be tapped. A study in Indonesia showed that production is 3 percent of what it could be. Iceland also has more potential. The Icelandic National Energy Authority says, "Only 20 to 25 percent of the technically and environmentally feasible hydropower and only 20 percent of the conventional geothermal potential available for electricity production in Iceland have been harnessed." In the United States, the Geological Survey estimates that less than 2 percent of potential geothermal energy is currently used.

Fifty Years of Progress

At the southwestern end of the Pacific rim, there is volcanic activity in New Zealand. The first geothermal plant was opened in 1957 in the Taupo volcanic zone of the North Island where magma rises close to the surface. This raises the temperature to at least 662°F (350°C) at depths of less than 3 miles (5 km). There are 29 geothermal areas here and 100 more in the rest of the country. Each field covers about 4.6 square miles (12 sq km). Many spout boiling water as well as steam. There are plans to build a geothermal plant 15.5 miles (25 km) from the Bay of Plenty on the Pacific Ocean. The Kawerau plant will be the largest geothermal power project in New Zealand since 1989. It will increase the country's geothermal capacity by 25 percent.

Overcoming Problems

Like all power plants, geothermal units can break down. This happened to an African geothermal generator, the 8.5 MW Aluto-Langano plant in Ethiopia. It started generating in 1999, but technical problems forced it to stop operation in 2002. While it is being repaired and checked, engineers are taking the opportunity to increase its production capacity to 30 MW.

Demonstrators protest against a geothermal project in Hawaii (see opposite).

No to Geo!

Building geothermal plants in national parks and places of scenic interest can divide public opinion. A project in Hawaii caused protests and demonstrations. Some protesters carried banners that read "Just say no to geo!" The project was a power plant planned for the 40 square mile (104 sq km) Wao Kele O Puna (green forest of Puna), the largest U.S. rainforest. Community groups gathered to protect the forest, which has been used for hunting, gathering, and religious purposes. It is also home to 200 native Hawaiian animal and plant species, including many considered endangered. In 2006, the Office of Hawaiian Affairs announced that it had bought the forest and that it would not be developed.

Geothermal Power in East Africa

The Great Rift Valley, in East Africa, is another region where moving plates have caused geothermal activity. The rift stretches for about 4,350 miles (7,000 km) where valleys are filled with lakes bounded by volcanic mountains. There is little geothermal power production in Africa, but Kenya and Ethiopia—both on the eastern branch of the rift—have opened plants.

The Olkaria power plant is made up of three units in Hell's Gate National Park near Kenya's Lake Naivasha. The first was opened in 1981. Today, 110 thermal wells have been drilled down to 4,265 feet (1,300 m). Altogether, the Olkaria geothermal field covers 27 square miles (70 sq km). The United Nations believes that geothermal energy in developing countries will reduce the need for fossil fuels or hydropower that can be affected by the dry season. Geothermal provides 11 percent of Kenya's power, and experts say there is the potential to generate much more.

Geothermal power production in the East African country of Kenya. Demand for electricity is growing at eight percent a year in Kenya. Energy experts predict that geothermal power will help to supply the increased demand.

What Does the Future Hold?

Experts agree that all renewable sources of energy —including geothermal—will become more important, and we will use them more in the future. Forecasts predict that demand for electricity will double over the next 25 years, stretching current resources.

Politicians want to convince voters that there will not be shortages of electricity or fuels, especially for transportation. At the same time, environmentalists continue to be concerned that energy policies do not increase pollution or contribute further to global warming. These concerns place geothermal power in a strong position compared with fossil fuels.

Improving the Technology

The technology of Enhanced Geothermal Systems (or EGS) includes Hot Dry Rock (HDR, see page 32). The systems are called enhanced (meaning increased) because they add water from the surface to the natural thermal water that is already underground. There are some concerns about this, especially the possibility of triggering earthquakes, (see page 33), but the technology will improve in the coming decades. There are EGS research projects in many parts of the world.

Time for Action

A group of experts at Massachusetts Institute of Technology (MIT) undertook a study of EGS in 2005. Their conclusion was that immediate action is needed: "Because prototype commercial-scale EGS will take a few years to develop and field-test, the time for action is now. Supporting the EGS program now will move us along the learning curve to a point where the design and engineering of well-connected EGS reservoir systems is technically reliable and reproducible . . . The payoff for EGS is

Members of the Australian Greens party dressed as lifesavers for a demonstration in Sydney. They want to save the planet by doing everything they can to prevent further global warming.

large, especially in the light of how much will have to be spent for deployment of conventional gas, nuclear, or coal-fired systems to meet replacement of retiring plants and capacity increases, as there are no other options with sufficient scale on the horizon . . . Like all new energy-supply technologies, for EGS to enter and compete in evolving U.S. electricity markets, positive policies at the state and federal levels will be required. These policies must be similar to those that oil and gas and other mineral-extraction operations have received in the past."

What About Cost?

People are concerned about the cost of energy, especially electricity. One of the problems with large geothermal projects is that the initial costs are high. This means that electricity from geothermal sources costs more to produce than electricity from sources such as fossil fuels. In some countries, geothermal and other renewable sources are helped to compete with fossil fuels by what is called a feed-in tariff. This is the price per unit of electricity that a national or regional energy supplier has to pay for renewable electricity (including geothermal) from private generators. The government sets the tariff (or price). In Germany, for example, this is covered by a Renewable Energy Law. This helps new energy-generating companies compete with traditional suppliers. Once the initial costs have been paid off, geothermal energy should be very cheap.

These heads of lettuce are growing in a geothermally heated greenhouse at Chena Hot Springs, Alaska. The greenhouse is near a low-temperature geothermal power plant (see panel opposite).

Using Waste Gas

A U.S. scientist has proposed pumping waste carbon dioxide (CO_2) gas into thermal reservoirs. Under high pressure, the CO_2 would act as a fluid and replace water in an HDR system (see page 32). The CO_2 would stay in a closed system and not escape into the air. The waste gas could come from sources such as coal- or gas-fired power stations. This use helps combat the greenhouse effect and global warming. The scientist has been granted a patent on his version of this process.

Community Projects

There could be many more small-scale community projects. One project opened in 2007 in Unterhaching, a town south of Munich in Germany. Thermal hot water is piped from 2 miles (3.3 km) underground to heat local houses. In Germany's capital, Berlin, the national parliament building has its own geothermal system. In summer, waste heat is

Low-Temperature Generation

In 2006, the Chena Hot Springs 400 kW generator in Alaska started making electricity from thermal water at a temperature lower than 165°F (74°C). This is the lowest temperature recorded in the world for geothermal electricity production. The Chena has reduced the cost of its power production in the region to one-fifth of what it had been with a diesel-fired generator.

pumped to a natural water reservoir in sandstone 1,050 feet (320 m) below ground. In winter, 158°F (70°C) hot water is brought up to heat the large building.

Make it International

Sharing information will help the development of geothermal technology, especially if industrialized countries share their knowledge with developing nations. The results of research and development can be shared through the International Geothermal Association (IGA). Founded in 1988, its headquarters is in Reykjavik, Iceland. The IGA has more than 2,000 members in 65 countries and has strong connections with the United Nations. The association organizes World Geothermal congresses. The next one is scheduled for 2010 in Bali, Indonesia.

Fuel Cells

Another development could be in hydrogen-powered fuel cells. These generate electricity to run vehicles such as cars. All that is needed are hydrogen and oxygen, with water as a harmless by-product. The problem is that it takes a lot of energy to split hydrogen from water or hydrocarbons. Scientists are finding ways of using geothermal power to provide this energy, which would make producing hydrogen easy and relatively cheap. This could be a major step in reducing fossil fuels burned for transport.

Planning a Mix of Energy Sources

After reading all the facts about geothermal power, including its potential, do you think this should be the sole solution to our energy needs in the future? Many experts believe it would be better to view it as one element in an energy mix of renewable resources (biomass, geothermal, solar, water, and wind) and nonrenewable sources (fossil fuels and nuclear energy). That way, we should avoid the possibility of an energy gap and make sure that the energy we use and the electricity we generate are less harmful to the environment.

Glossary

asthenosphere   A zone in the upper part of Earth's mantle.

carbon dioxide (CO_2)   A greenhouse gas given off when fossil fuels are burned.

climate change   A change in general weather conditions over a long period of time including higher temperatures, more or less rain, droughts, etc.

condense   To change from a gas into a liquid (as steam into water).

conductor   A substance that allows something such as heat to pass along or through it.

constructive margin   A divergent margin.

continental plate   A tectonic plate beneath the land of a continent.

convergent margin   A boundary between tectonic plates where one plate dips beneath another.

derrick   A framework that supports drilling equipment.

destructive margin   A convergent margin.

divergent margin   A boundary between tectonic plates where new crust is formed.

dormant   Inactive.

dynamo   A machine that turns mechanical energy into electrical energy.

electromagnetic induction   The process of creating electricity by using magnetic forces.

emission   Producing and giving off something (such as a waste gas); also, the waste gas produced and given off.

fumarole   A hole in the ground that releases geothermal steam and volcanic gases.

geologist   A scientist who studies the structure of Earth.

geyser   A hot spring where boiling water and steam regularly shoot up high in the air.

global warming   Heating up of Earth's surface, especially caused by pollution from burning fossil fuels.

greenhouse effect   Warming of Earth's surface caused especially by pollution from burning fossil fuels.

greenhouse gas   A gas, such as carbon dioxide, that traps heat from the Sun near Earth and helps to create the greenhouse effect.

hydrogen sulfide   A flammable gas with a characteristic smell of rotten eggs.

isobutane   A gaseous substance that can be used as a fuel.

magma   Molten rock formed in Earth's mantle.

mantle   The thick layer of molten rock beneath Earth's crust.

mechanical energy   The energy that something has because of its position (potential energy) and its movement (kinetic energy). Also, the energy transmitted by a machine.

mineral   A solid chemical substance that occurs naturally in Earth.

mud pot   A place where geothermal steam bubbles through a surface layer of mud.

nickel   A hard silver-white metal.

nitric oxide   A colorless poisonous gas.

ocean crust   Earth's crust beneath an ocean.

oceanic plate   A tectonic plate beneath the waters of an ocean.

radioactive decay   The process by which substances with unstable atoms (such as uranium) give off energy.

renewable resources   Sources of energy that do not run out by being used, such as biomass, geothermal, solar, water, and wind power.

Richter scale   A scale from 1 to 10 used to measure the strength of earthquakes.

scrubber   A device that filters and cleans harmful fumes.

silica   A hard mineral (silicon dioxide).

subduction zone   The region of a convergent margin where one tectonic plate dips beneath another.

tectonic plate   One of the large pieces of Earth's crust.

United Nations   An international organization that promotes peace and security.

uranium   A radioactive metal that is used to produce nuclear power.

vaporize   To change into a vapor (or gas).

Web Sites

The International Geothermal Association (IGA) Facts, Data, and Opinions
http://iga.igg.cnr.it

U.S. Department of Energy's Geothermal Technologies Program
www1.eere.energy.gov/geothermal

Geothermal Energy Association: Environmental Benefits of Geothermal Energy
www.geo-energy.org/aboutGE/environment.asp#airemissions

Case Study: Geothermal Energy in Erding, Germany
www.managenergy.net/products/R444.htm

Index

CHOO CHOO

SIZZLE

SIZZLE

KNOCK

KNOCK

POP

POP

BUZZ

BUZZ

BUZZ

MOO

KLOPP

KLOPP

SLURP

SLURP

SLURP

Mr. Brown Can MOO! Can You?

By Dr. Seuss

Random House 🏠 New York

Published in the United States by Random House Children's Books,
a division of Random House, Inc., New York.

Random House and colophon are registered trademarks of Random House, Inc.

www.randomhouse.com/kids
www.seussville.com
www.kohlscorporation.com

Educators and librarians, for a variety of teaching tools, visit us at
www.randomhouse.com/teachers

This special edition was printed for Kohl's by Random House Children's Books,
a division of Random House, Inc., New York.

ISBN: 978-0-375-85378-4

MANUFACTURED IN CHINA
10 9 8 7 6 5 4 3 2 1

Random House Children's Books supports the First Amendment
and celebrates the right to read.

Oh, the wonderful things
Mr. Brown can do!
He can go like a cow.
He can go MOO MOO
Mr. Brown can do it.
How about you?

He can go like a bee.

Mr. Brown can

BUZZ

How about you?
Can you go

BUZZ
BUZZ

He can go
like a cork . . .

He can go like horse feet

He can go

EEK EEK

like a squeaky shoe.

He can go
like a rooster . . .

COCK A DOODLE DOO

He can go
like an owl . . .

Hoo Hoo
Hoo Hoo

Eek Eek
Eek Eek
Cock-a-Doodle-Doo
Hoo Hoo   Hoo Hoo

How about you?

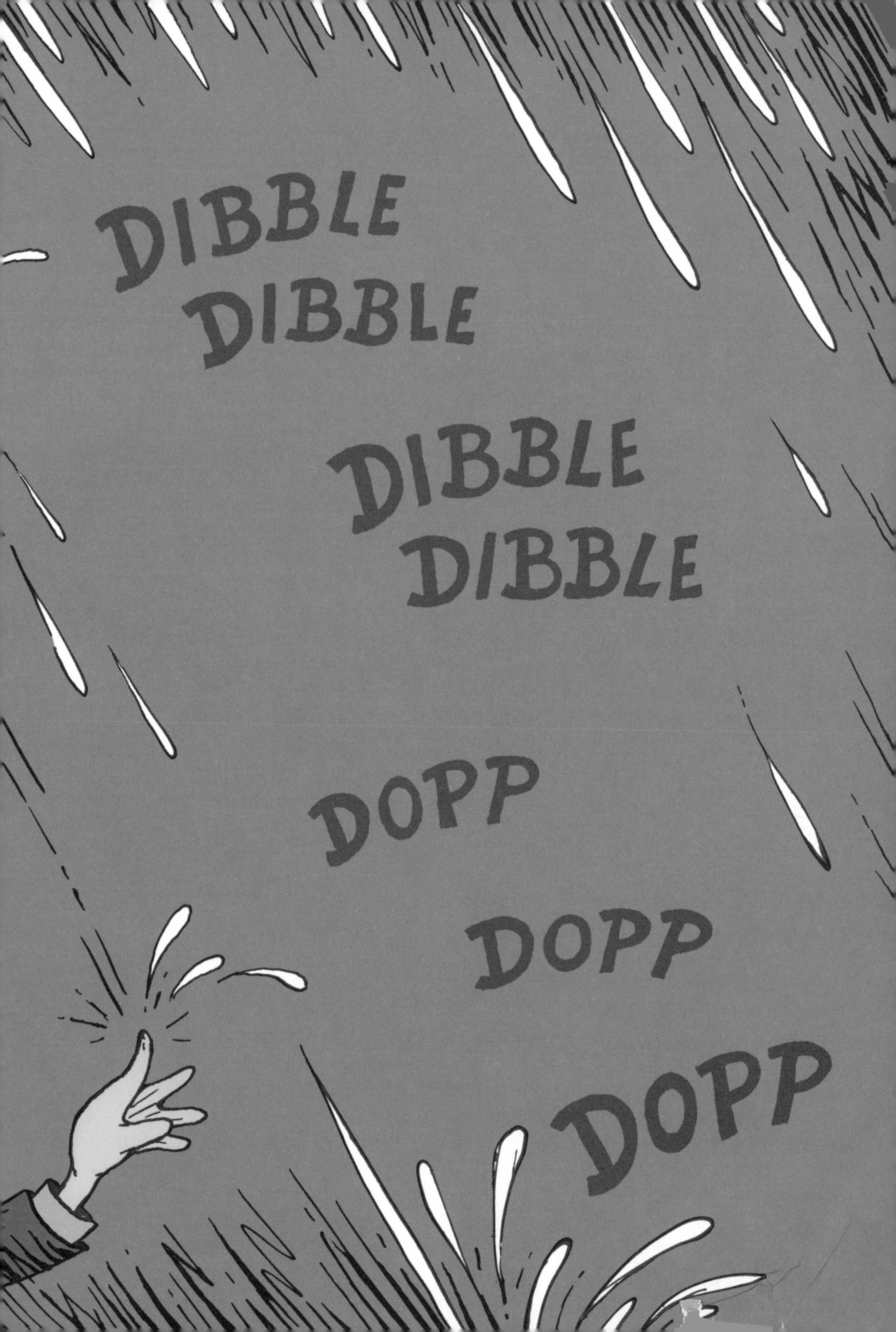
DIBBLE
DIBBLE
DIBBLE
DIBBLE
DOPP
DOPP
DOPP

He can go like a train

CHOO CHOO
CHOO
CHOO

Oh, the wonderful things
Mr. Brown can do!

Moo Moo
Buzz Buzz
Pop Pop Pop
Eek Eek
Hoo Hoo
Klopp Klopp Klopp
Dibble Dibble
Dopp Dopp
Cock-a-Doodle-Doo

Mr. Brown can do it.
How about you?

Mr. Brown
can

WHISPER WHISPER

. . . very soft
very high . . .

. . . like the soft,
soft whisper
of a butterfly.

Maybe YOU can, too.
I think you ought to try.

He can go
like a horn . . .

. . . like a big cat drinking

SLURP
SLURP
SLURP

He can go like a clock.
He can

TICK

He can

TOCK

He can go
like a hand
on a door . . .

Oh, the wonderful things
Mr. Brown can do!

BLURP BLURP
SLURP SLURP

COCK-A-DOODLE-DOO

KNOCK KNOCK KNOCK

and HOO HOO HOO

He can even

SIZZLE
SIZZLE

He can do that, too,
like an egg
in a frying pan.
How about you?

Mr. Brown is smart,
as smart as they come!
He can do
a hippopotamus
chewing gum!

GRUM

GRUM

GRUM

GRUM

GRUM
GRUM
GRUM

Mr. Brown is
so smart
he can even do this:
he can even
make a noise
like a goldfish kiss!

BOOM BOOM BOOM

Mr. Brown is a wonder!

BOOM BOOM BOOM

Mr. Brown makes thunder!

He makes lightning!

SPLATT SPLATT SPLATT

And it's very, very hard
to make a noise like that.

Oh, the wonderful things
Mr. Brown can do!

Moo Moo
Buzz Buzz
Pop Pop Pop

   Eek Eek
   Hoo Hoo
   Klopp Klopp Klopp

Dibble Dibble
Dopp Dopp
Cock-a-Doodle-Doo

   Grum Grum
   Grum Grum
   Choo Choo Choo

Boom Boom
Splatt Splatt
Tick Tick Tock

   Sizzle Sizzle
   Blurp Blurp
   Knock Knock Knock

A SLURP and a WHISPER
and a FISH KISS, too.

Mr. Brown can do it.
How about YOU?

EEK EEK

COCK A
DOODLE
DOO

M BOOM BOOM

BLURP
BLURP

DIBBLE
DIBBLE

DOPP

DOPP

GRUM
GRUM

DOPP

SPLATT SPLATT SPLATT

HOO
HOO

TICK TOCK
TICK TOCK